TIPTOE THROUGH THE
T-U-L-I-Ps
but try to keep your balance!

CALVINISM · ARMINIANISM · BIBLICAL

DR. ARV EDGEWORTH

TIPTOE THROUGH THE
T-U-L-I-Ps

but try to keep your balance!

CALVINISM · ARMINIANISM · BIBLICAL

DR. ARV EDGEWORTH

Copyright © 2009 Arv Edgeworth. All rights reserved. Writings contained herein are by the author unless otherwise stated.

No part of this publication may be reproduced, stored in a retrieval system or transmitted in any way by any means – electronic, mechanical, photocopy, recording or otherwise – without the prior permission of the copyright holder, except as provided by USA copyright law.

All Scriptures are taken from the King James Bible. Portions of verses in **bold** indicate emphasis added by the author.

ISBN# 978-1-935075-52-3

Printed in the United States of America.

Printed by Calvary Publishing
A Ministry of Parker Memorial Baptist Church
1902 East Cavanaugh Road
Lansing, Michigan 48910
www.CalvaryPublishing.org

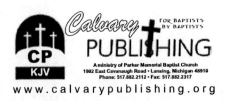

ACKNOWLEDGEMENTS 7
INTRODUCTION 9

PART ONE - *Arminianism*

CHAPTER ONE
I Thought I Had Sinned But I Made A Mistake 15

CHAPTER TWO
But, Can You Ever Be Sure, In The Twilight Zone? . . . 23

CHAPTER THREE
Oh Yeah, There Was Old Ernie on T.V. 27

CHAPTER FOUR
Oh No! Please God, Make the Preacher Choke or
Something! 33

CHAPTER FIVE
Five Reasons Why the Believer Is Forever Secure . . . 37

CHAPTER SIX
Problem Texts Concerning the Believer's Security 53

PART TWO - *Calvinism*

CHAPTER SEVEN
The Five Points of Calvinism 77

CHAPTER EIGHT
Ten Scriptural Errors Of Calvinism 83

CHAPTER NINE
Dear Calvinistic Friend 107

CHAPTER TEN
The Tale of Two Systems 111

ACKNOWLEDGEMENTS

I want to thank Mr. Gar Jex, and Mr. Roger Haskins for their editing and comments in the writing of this book.

INTRODUCTION

On August 2, 1968, at about 1:00 in the morning, I made the greatest and most important decision that I will ever make in my life. That night I realized that I needed Jesus Christ in my life, and without Him I was a sinner on my way to a place called hell. I asked Him to save me that night and He did.

About two years later my wife and I became members of a church that is part of a group of churches that is referred to as the Holiness Movement. This group includes the Wesleyan, Free Methodist, Nazarene, United Brethren, and a few other churches. These churches believe that after you are saved you need to seek a second work of grace in your life called "entire sanctification." When a believer reached this second spiritual plateau, many in this group at one time believed the believer no longer possessed a sin nature.

These churches still believe that once you are saved, it is possible that you can backslide, fall back into sin, and thereby lose your salvation. They teach that God will keep us, only if we want to be kept. This teaching is called Arminianism, after the teachings of Jacobus Arminius, a Dutch Protestant theologian of the late 16th century (1560-1609).

In 1978, I began a two year spiritual struggle over these teachings of the movement. My struggle began with having a sincere desire to have a better

10

understanding of the doctrine of entire sanctification so that I might be better equipped to defend this position scripturally. But more and more, I kept finding statements by their writers which I considered to be unscriptural.

During my search for truth, I came upon an alternate position, which is referred to as the five points of Calvinism, after the teachings of John Calvin (1509-1564), a French theologian and religious reformer that lived in Switzerland.

Calvin's teachings on election and predestination are also referred to as the TULIP THEORY. As I studied Calvinism's teachings, once again I kept finding more and more statements that I considered to be unscriptural. The Arminians put much emphasis on man's free will, and little on the Sovereignty of God. The Calvinists put much emphasis on the Sovereignty of God, but little if any at all on man's free will. But if both are clearly taught in the Bible, then there should be a balanced viewpoint.

The one thing I noticed about most churches where either extreme position was taught, few people were being saved on a regular basis, and little effort was being made to reach them. But in churches that seemed to be alive and where people were being saved, there was usually a very balanced viewpoint towards God's Sovereignty and the free will of man.

I would like to share with you some of the things I struggled with concerning these two extreme doctrines. Whether or not you agree with my conclusions, it is my desire that through this book each of us might have a greater desire to praise and serve God because of His wonderful salvation that He has provided through the Lord Jesus Christ.

In His Service
Arv Edgeworth

PART ONE
Arminianism

CHAPTER ONE

I Thought I Had Sinned, But I Made A Mistake

IN 1978, I began a two-year search for truth that ended with my family and I leaving the church we had been a part of for ten years. It was not an easy decision. This was the only church that our three children had ever known. Most of our friends were there.

My search actually started because one year earlier I had been elected to the position of Sunday School Superintendent. I finally decided I needed to get a better understanding of the doctrine of "Entire Sanctification," which is also sometimes referred to as "Christian Perfection," or the "Second Blessing." This is very similar to the experience that the Pentecostals believe in, only without being accompanied by "Speaking in Tongues." One of the

16   Tiptoe Through the T-U-L-I-Ps

Holiness doctrinal books on sanctification actually quotes a Pentecostal preacher in his description of how to prepare yourself to receive the experience.

When I began my search, I started checking out of our church library every book that dealt with the subject. One of the first books I studied was entirely scripture arranged under different headings that was to cover every aspect of the doctrine. So I wrote all the verses down under the different headings, and looked all the passages up in the Bible. I was going to pick out only the best verses under each heading, making sure there wasn't anything taken out of context. I'd just circle the best ones. I wanted to be ready when those Baptists came around. Those Baptists were a tough bunch. They always had all those Bible verses to back up what they believed. Well, I would be ready now.

Much to my dismay, I wasn't able to circle any verses under the first heading. They were not very clear, and I wasn't sure what was really implied. Oh well, this was just the first aspect of the doctrine, and a minor point anyway, let's go on to the main headings.

It wasn't getting any better. I had to keep writing, "not clear," or "not implied," or just put a question mark. When I finished the book, I only had about six verses circled, and I realized they were really so weak they wouldn't hold up under scrutiny. It just wasn't

but try to keep your balance!   17

clear enough what they really meant. Now what was I going to do? I didn't have any Bible verses to stand on. So I started studying all the books by early leaders of the movement, plus all the current writers.

At first I found several good statements that I eagerly wrote down. But soon my own notes were becoming more and more negative. There were just too many statements that I could not accept as being scriptural. Here are some of the beliefs I was having a problem accepting.

The churches in the Holiness Movement at that time believed in the "eradication of our sin nature."

Eradication means:

- Get entirely rid of; destroy completely.
- Pull out by the roots.

They believed that this happened when a believer was entirely sanctified. This experience was described in such terms as:

- "purification of the heart from even inherited depravity"
- "cleansed of the carnal nature"
- "the sin nature is gone"
- "the removal of temptation from within"
- "they are perfect as not to commit sin"
- "freed from evil desires and tempers"
- "a constantly existing state of perfected holiness"

18   TIPTOE THROUGH THE T-U-L-I-PS

They believed that you prepare yourself for attaining this experience by:

- "a zealous keeping of all the commandments"
- "watchfulness and painfulness"
- "denying ourselves and taking up our cross daily"
- "earnest prayer and fasting"
- "close attendance on all the ordinances of God"

After you do all of the above, you are ready for God to "entirely sanctify" you in a single moment, in reward for you so fervently seeking the experience. But, once you receive it, you must continue to do all of the things listed above, or you may lose the experience.

Since they believe that a person who has this experience does not commit sin, then they must have quite a problem when one of them does something wrong. Right? Wrong! They teach that although we "make **mistakes** in judgment and **practice**," and these various defects are **"deviations from the perfect law,"** and they even admit that these **"need an atonement."** However, since an entirely sanctified person's sole motivation is love, then these **"mistakes"** could not **"in the scriptural sense be sin."** (Oh I get it. I thought I had sinned, but I made a

but try to keep your balance! 19

mistake.) You see, if they did not teach this, then they would have to admit that they still had a sin nature.

Another thing that I had trouble accepting was that many of them, including my former pastor, did not believe in a "positional sanctification." That is that believers are positionally "saints" and "holy" from the moment of believing. Many of them claimed that Baptists believe "only" in a "positional sanctification."

Some examples of "positional sanctification" are:

- "Unto the church of God which is at Corinth, to them that are **sanctified in Christ Jesus…**" (First Corinthians 1:2)
- "…unto the church of God which is at Corinth, with all the **saints** which are in all Achaia:" (Second Corinthians 1:1)
- "…to the **saints** which are at Ephesus…" (Ephesians 1:1)
- "…to all the **saints in Christ Jesus** which are at Philippi…" (Philippians 1:1)
- "Wherefore, **holy brethren**…" (Hebrews 3:1)
- "…to them that are **sanctified** by God the Father, and preserved in Jesus Christ…" (Jude 1)

The New Testament writers were not just addressing themselves to only the more mature believers, or even to a select group of Christians who had received something that other believers in the same cities hadn't, when they used the terms: "sanctified, holy brethren, saints;" but rather they were referring to something that every believer has "in Christ." They were referring to their "position," rather than their "practice."

Another claim that they made was that the Holy Spirit is a comforter only for those who have been "entirely sanctified." They teach that the Holy Spirit is only "with" the believer, but "in" the "entirely sanctified."

The more books I read, the more claims I found that I could not accept as being scriptural. I finally talked to my pastor one day about some of the statements I had been reading. After taking a deep breath he said, "To be honest with you, some of our early church leaders didn't always possess everything that they professed."

That helped for awhile, but after reading many books by then current writers, along with our Sunday School teaching manuals on the subject, it seemed that the weight on my chest was getting heavier and heavier. I was becoming more and more convinced, that we were teaching a mystical experience for which there was really no scriptural ba-

but try to keep your balance! 21

sis. Whenever there was special preaching on the experience, many people were not 100% sure that they still had the experience, or even if they really ever had it to begin with. Personally, I believed that I must have received the experience at salvation, because my heart attitude was right at the time (I was told that was possible). And because I had walked close with the Lord, and remained yielded to Him, I had never had much doubt that I must have had it. But how could I be sure?

CHAPTER TWO

But, Can You Ever Be Sure, In The Twilight Zone?

As TIME went on, I became more and more uncertain about the reality of an experience called "entire sanctification." Several other young couples were having similar doubts about the beliefs of the church at the same time. I was not aware of this at first, but, finally one of the men, a close friend, who was one of our Sunday School teachers, came to me and admitted his own doubts about the doctrine. Later, during the fall quarter, we were going to be teaching this in our adult classes. After several discussions on the subject, he asked me, "What are we going to do, we can't teach this stuff?"

I didn't really have an answer for him. But more and more the atmosphere surrounding this experience seemed like, "nu nu, nu nu, nu nu, nu nu … You are now entering another dimension. Maybe you have the experience and maybe you don't. But, can you ever be sure, in the Twilight Zone?"

About this time I asked my pastor if I could meet with him, I needed to talk. After discussing my feelings with him he said, "I have a book at the parsonage that I think will help." Although, after one of my statements he said, "That sounds almost Calvinistic." He believed all Baptists were basically Calvinists. Later, I was to find out that all Baptists were not Calvinists, but at the time I wasn't even sure what a Calvinist was.

I eagerly accepted the offer of the book and went home to begin studying it. Maybe this was what we were looking for, a more balanced practical viewpoint. However, this was not the case. In the book I found nineteen more statements I could not accept as being scriptural. One of the claims was that only a sanctified person is sealed with the Holy Spirit. But according to (Ephesians 1:13-14), this happens to every believer the moment we trust Christ as our Saviour.

But the claim I objected to the most was that our continued forgiveness for our past sins is conditioned upon our spirit of forgiveness toward those that sin against us. I showed this to my wife Marti and we both said, "That's not what the Bible says,

but try to keep your balance! 25

how can they make that statement?" All of this added together made me realize I could not accept their
doctrine anymore. I knew I would have to look in
another direction for truth, but where?

CHAPTER THREE

Oh Yeah, There Was Old Ernie on T.V.
(Not his real name.)

I KNEW now what I was going to have to do, but it wasn't going to be easy. I no longer had any faith in this denomination, and it wasn't going to be long before I would have to leave.

Where would we go? I didn't know if I could accept what the Baptists taught about the "Eternal Security of the believer." That is, once you are saved, you are saved forever, no matter what. I remember an Arminian pastor telling my wife and I, when we were just baby Christians, "Well, you know what those Baptists believe. They teach that once you are saved, you can go out and live any way you want to, and you will still go to heaven." Later I was to find out that wasn't exactly the way the Baptists taught it; well, most of them anyway.

I knew I couldn't accept what the Pentecostals believe, so where could we go? Was there a middle ground somewhere between the Arminians and the Baptists? Finally I decided to find out what the Baptists believed about "sanctification." Much to my surprise, it was exactly what I had come to believe through my own personal study of the Scriptures.

Well, now what? So I decided to check out "Eternal Security" in the Bible. First, what did Jesus say in the four gospels? As I studied what Jesus taught about salvation and the conditions involved, I just kept finding one positive statement after another, "...**have** eternal life..." "...**has** everlasting life..." "...shall **never** perish..." Where were the conditions, "If you continue to do this," or, "If you don't do that..."? With anything as important as this, if there were conditions for keeping it involved, wouldn't Jesus have said so?

So then I decided to study all the verses that the Arminians use to prove that a Christian can lose his salvation. As I studied the passages these verses were taken from, considering who the passage was addressed to, what they were talking about, and so on, I realized that many of them were taken out of context, and almost all of them could easily be explained away. So once again I was left without any real verses to stand on.

Now I began to study many of the great doctrines

but try to keep your balance! 29

that were related to salvation, such as justification, sanctification, adoption, etc., and as I did so, I saw them for the first time in light of the believer's security in Christ. It was as if a veil had been lifted from my eyes. For the first time I could understand truths from the Bible that before had been somewhat hazy in my understanding. Everything I studied now was like a breath of fresh air. Praise God for His wonderful grace!

It was about this time that I knew that I wanted my family and I to be a part of a good soul-winning Baptist church somewhere. But I remembered back to quite some time before this, when at that time I still believed in the teachings of the Holiness Movement, that I thought to myself one day, "Wouldn't it be great to be a Baptist and be a part of a great soul-winning church somewhere? Wouldn't it be great to be identified with some of the great preachers who were Baptists, like Dr. John R. Rice, and Dr. Jack Hyles, and oh yeah, there was old Ernie on TV. I think he's supposed to be a Baptist." I didn't know then that old Ernie (not his real name) would decide to change camps.

Actually I had learned about them from reading the Sword of the Lord paper. My wife and I had been saved while attending a church that was Baptistic in doctrine, but we had moved to another area soon after that and ended up in that Arminian church. But someone from our old church had turned our name in for a gift subscription to the Sword paper. I remember once turning in a list of twenty-five names and addresses for a few sample issues of the Sword of the Lord while at the Arminian church. Wow, what an uproar that caused. The pastor made a rather harsh inquiry from the pulpit about the matter after he had received a lot of angry complaints. Of course I had turned his name and address in too. He never did find out who did it, but I think later he might have had a pretty good idea who the culprit was. I guessed I should have confessed the day I left the church, just to ease his mind about whether the guy was still there or not.

Finally when I couldn't take it any longer, knowing that I did not believe the way they did, and not really wanting my family to be influenced any longer by their teachings, I talked to my wife about it first, then that Sunday afternoon we sat our kids down in the living room, and let them know of the decision. I explained to them how I felt, and told them that I wanted to hand in my resignation, and leave the church.

Although this wasn't going to be easy, leaving all our friends, and our church family, my wife told me that whatever I decided was best for our family, she would agree to. Praise God for the wonderful wife He has given me. She is always there in every

but try to keep your balance! 31

important decision that has to be made, supporting me and trying to help in any way she can. I guess it was a little easier because she had known how miserable I had been for several months, agonizing over this decision.

That afternoon, about 5:00 p.m., I walked up to the front door of the parsonage and rang the doorbell. As I talked with the man who had been my pastor for ten years, and had also been my friend, it was probably the hardest thing I had ever had to do in my life. I told him I had prayed much about this, and although it was hard, I knew I could no longer stay in the Holiness Movement. I gave him a statement that I had written out, explaining my reasons for doing so scripturally. I asked him to read it to the church board, although I was sure that he wouldn't. The last thing I asked him was, "Pastor, if I were to live holy for the rest of my life, but just before I died, or just before the Lord came back, I had a sinful thought, and I didn't ask for forgiveness, would I go to heaven?" He thought hard for a moment, then after taking a deep breath he said, "No, I don't think so." I said, "Pastor, I believe God's grace goes a lot farther than that." With that I shook his hand and said good-bye.

What a relief I felt come over me as I drove home. It was as if a huge weight had been lifted off my chest. Praise God, I felt like a new man. I couldn't wait to start looking for a good Baptist church to attend. I thought to myself, "I wonder how far it is to old Ernie's church? Maybe we could at least visit once."

CHAPTER FOUR

Oh No! Please God, Make the Preacher Choke or Something!

THE NEXT Sunday we decided we would visit a Baptist church in another town, we lived almost in the middle between the two towns anyway. The Sunday School class went pretty good, although they did look at me kind of funny when I made a comment about Christ keeping us. But I couldn't believe the preaching service. It was cold, dead, stuffy, and formal. The special number by the soloist was actually pretty good. One older gentleman even offered a weak "Amen." But everything in the whole service was outlined in the bulletin, and I mean everything! They told you when to stand up, what to sing, when to sit down, what to say. I remember leaning over and whispering quietly into my wife's ear, "It doesn't say when we can clear our

34 TIPTOE THROUGH THE T-U-L-I-PS

throat." Although I'm not sure it was allowed during the service anyway.

Then came the message. For the next two hours (it seemed like), the preacher told us how we could lose our salvation. I remember thinking: "Oh no! Please God, make the preacher choke or something!" This was exactly what I didn't want my family to hear. I couldn't wait to get out of there. We were going on vacation the following week, so we decided to have church at home that night, and then we would start looking again when we got back.

The first Sunday we were on vacation we tried the Baptist church in a nearby town. The Sunday School class was good as before. Yet, there seemed to be something different this time. The church had a new pastor that had just been there a few weeks. Praise God, that morning my family and I heard the first in a series of messages he was to preach on "The Grace of God."

What a blessing that was. My wife thought it was a good message too. For the next few weeks after our vacation we visited other Baptist churches in the area. We finally decided on one, and after visiting for a few weeks we decided to join. We were to stay there for two years until the pastor left. Then God would lead us to Trinity Baptist Church in Flushing, Michigan. What a blessing it has been for our family to serve under the ministry of Dr. Leonard Saunders.

but try to keep your balance! 35

We have been there over twenty-five years now. We are now in our third building program as the church has gone from about 30 people to 600-700 under Dr. Saunders' leadership.

The Holiness movement doesn't take the exact same stand today on the sin nature of an entirely sanctified Christian. The early leaders spoke of the total eradication and removal of the sin nature at entire sanctification. Today they speak in terms of it being rendered powerless, not completely removed. That is basically what Baptists believe happens as we yield to the Holy Spirit's power in our life.

But the one major point of difference that separates us from the Arminians, is the eternal security of the believer.

CHAPTER FIVE

Five Reasons Why the Believer Is Forever Secure

REASON #1
Because the Believer Is Not Under Law,
But Under Grace

A number of years ago I was having a conversation with a man I worked with that went to a church that believed you can lose your salvation. I asked him this question, "If I were not saved, and I kept the 10 Commandments my whole life the best I knew how, would I go to heaven?" He said, "Absolutely not! You have to trust in Jesus Christ to forgive your sins. Keeping the 10 Commandments won't get you to heaven." So far we both agreed.

Then I asked him, "Let's say that I get saved, then just before I die I murder someone and don't repent of it, will I go to heaven?" He said, "I don't think so."

37

38 TIPTOE THROUGH THE T-U-L-I-PS

I said, "Wait a minute, you just said keeping the 10 Commandments won't get me to heaven, but now you say if I break one of them it will send me to hell? Does my going to heaven depend on keeping the 10 Commandments or not?" At that point he was a bit confused. One of the reasons he was confused was because he didn't have a proper understanding of God's grace.

Grace means "unmerited favor." Ephesians 2:8-9 says: "For by **grace** are ye saved through faith; and that **not of yourselves**: *it is* the gift of God: **Not of works**, lest any man should boast." If we could get to heaven by keeping the 10 Commandments, or doing a lot of good deeds, then we could earn our own salvation. If that were true, why would Jesus have to die?

Many people believe when they get to heaven there will be a giant scale up there. All our good works will be placed on one side, and all our bad works placed on the other. If our good works out-weigh our bad we will be allowed into heaven. The problem with that is, the Bible says we are not saved by our works. Titus 3:5 says: "**Not by works of righteousness which we have done**, but according to his mercy he saved us…"

Grace is the very opposite of human merit, or good works. Romans 11:6 says: "And if by **grace**, then *is it* no more of **works**: otherwise grace is no

but try to keep your balance! 39

more grace. But if *it be* of **works**, then is it no more **grace**: otherwise work is no more work."

However, grace is not hindered by **human demerit.** The fact that we are a sinner is the occasion for grace to do its work. If we could get to heaven by our own efforts in some way, we wouldn't need God's grace. If we have no sin, we don't need God's grace either. Another reason my friend was confused was because he didn't have a proper understanding of our relationship to God's law.

First let's define what we mean by God's law. Romans 7:7 says: "What shall we say then? *Is* the law sin? God forbid. Nay, I had not known sin, but by the law: for I had not known lust, except the law had said, Thou shalt not covet." So by the law we mean God's 10 Commandment law.

The Christian will no longer be judged by whether he keeps God's 10 Commandments or not. Romans 6:14 says: "For sin shall not have dominion over you: for ye are not **under the law**, but **under grace.**"

Romans 4:15 says, "Because the law worketh wrath: for **where no law is, *there is* no transgression.**" What that means is, if we go out on the highway and go 90 miles an hour and the speed limit sign says the limit is 70 miles an hour, we have transgressed, or broken the law. To transgress means to go beyond a boundary. However, if you live in a country that has no speed limit, then at 90 miles an hour you haven't broken any law. Actually, 71 mph is breaking the law.

The purpose of God's 10 Commandment law was two-fold: first, to expose sin. Romans 3:20 says: "Therefore by the deeds of the law there shall no flesh be justified in his sight: [we are not justified by keeping the 10 Commandments] **for by the law *is* the knowledge of sin.**" See also (Romans 7:7).

The second purpose for the law was to show us our need of a Saviour. Galatians 3:24 says, "Wherefore the law was our schoolmaster *to bring us* unto Christ, that we might be justified by faith." Possibly the most important purpose for God's 10 Commandments was to prove to us that we couldn't keep them, thus showing our need of a Saviour.

Christ delivered us from the law

Ephesians 2:12-16 says, "That at that time ye were without Christ, being aliens from the commonwealth of Israel, and strangers from the covenants of promise, having no hope, and without God in the world: But now in Christ Jesus ye who sometimes were far off are made nigh by the blood of Christ. For he is our peace, who hath made both one, and hath broken down the middle wall of partition between us; **Having abolished in his flesh** the enmity, even **the law of commandments** con-

but try to keep your balance! 41

tained in ordinances; for to make in himself of twain one new man, so making peace; And that he might reconcile both unto God in one body by the cross, **having slain the enmity thereby**:"

Colossians 2:13-14 says, "And you, being dead in your sins and the uncircumcision of your flesh, hath he quickened together with him, having **forgiven you all trespasses**; Blotting out the **handwriting of ordinances that was against us**, which was contrary to us, and **took it out of the way, nailing it to his cross**;"

We will no longer be judged in relation to God's 10 Commandment laws.

REASON #2
Because God Has Declared the Believer Not Guilty

A third reason my friend was confused was because he didn't have a proper understanding of "justification." Romans 5:1 says, "Therefore being justified by faith, we have peace with God through our Lord Jesus Christ:"

Three possible legal declarations concerning an accused person are:

- You are guilty, and you will be punished.
- You are guilty, but you will be pardoned.
- You are not guilty.

To be declared not guilty means that it was found that they did not commit the crime they were accused of. That is what "justified" means. God in His mercy and grace not only forgives us for our transgressions, He declares we never committed them. The reason He can do that is because someone else has already been declared guilty of our crimes, and punished for them; the Lord Jesus Christ.

First John 1:9 says, "If we confess our sins, he is faithful and just to forgive us *our* sins, and to cleanse us from all unrighteousness." First, the Bible says God is "faithful" to forgive our sins. That means if you do your part, He will do His part. Secondly, the Bible says God is "just" to forgive us our sins. If Jesus had not died and paid the price for our sins, we could pray to God and admit our guilt, and ask for His forgiveness and God could say, "Why should I forgive you. You did it, and you will pay for it." But because someone else has already been punished for our sins, God can freely forgive them when we ask Him to.

First John 2:2 says, "And he is the propitiation for our sins: and not for ours only, but also for *the sins of* the whole world." Propitiation means "to satisfy completely." God's justice was completely satisfied. The price has been paid in full.

Some have said, "Well I understand that God forgave my past sins, but what about the ones I haven't

but try to keep your balance! 43

committed yet?" When you asked Jesus to save you and forgive your sins, which sins did you ask forgiveness for? Which sins did He pay for? When He died on the cross, all our sins were future.

Romans 8:33-34 says, "Who shall lay any thing to the charge of God's elect? *It is* God that justifieth. Who *is* he that condemneth? *It is* Christ that died, yea rather, that is risen again, who is even at the right hand of God, who also maketh intercession for us."

God is the one we sin against, if anyone has a reason to hold us accountable He surely does; yet He declares us to be not guilty, dare anyone else lay any charge against us? Jesus died for us and Romans 8:35 says nothing can separate us from His love. In fact, rather than bring a charge against us, the Bible says He is our "advocate," or defense attorney that is there at the throne speaking out on our behalf.

First John 2:1, "My little children, these things write I unto you, that ye sin not. And if any man sin, we have an advocate with the Father, Jesus Christ the righteous:"

REASON #3
Because God Will Not Impute Sin to the Believer

A fourth reason my friend was confused was because he didn't have a proper understanding of "imputation." Romans 5:13 says, "(For until the law sin was in the world: but sin is not imputed when there

44   Tiptoe Through the T-U-L-I-Ps

is no law." Imputation means "to give credit or blame for something," or to "place on one's account."

Have you ever been given credit for something good that you didn't do? Have you ever been blamed for something bad that you didn't do? Sometimes people have to pay for crimes they didn't commit.

There are four kinds of imputation mentioned in the Bible:

1. Adam's sin was imputed to the human race.

M.G. Easton said, "…the sin of Adam is imputed to all his descendants, i.e., it is reckoned as theirs, and they are dealt with therefore as guilty;"

The Illustrated Bible Dictionary, by M.G. Easton,Thomas Nelson, [1897]

Romans 5:12, "Wherefore, as by one man sin entered into the world, and death by sin; and so death passed upon all men, for that all have sinned:"

Romans 5:18-19, "Therefore as by the offence of one *judgment came* upon all men to condemnation…For as by one man's disobedience many were made sinners…"

Matthew Henry said, "Adam sinning, his nature became guilty and corrupted, and so came to his children. Thus in him all have sinned. And death is by sin; for death is the wages of sin. Then entered all that misery which is the due desert of sin; temporal, spiritual, eternal death."

A.T. Robertson said, "The general point is plain

but try to keep your balance! 45

that the effects of Adam's sin are transmitted to his descendants, though he does not say how it was done whether by the natural or the federal headship of Adam."

C.H. Spurgeon said, "Here we find an explanation of the position of Adam in reference to the race of man. He represented us all, and we all share the sad effects of his transgression... All men sinned in Adam who stood as representative for them all, and therefore all men die."

William Burkitt said, "For as the disobedience of the first Adam is meritoriously imputed to all his natural posterity, and brings death upon all;"

You might be thinking, "That's not fair, Adam's sin was meritoriously imputed to us and placed on our account." Wait until you hear about the second kind of imputation.

2. The sin of the human race was imputed to Christ.

M.G. Easton said, "our sins are imputed to Christ, i.e., he assumed our "law-place," undertook to answer the demands of justice for our sins."

The Illustrated Bible Dictionary, by M.G. Easton, Thomas Nelson, [1897]

Second Corinthians 5:21, "For he hath made him *to be* sin for us, who knew no sin..." First Peter 2:24, "Who his own self bare our sins in his own body on the tree..."

46   TIPTOE THROUGH THE T-U-L-I-PS

3. Christ's righteousness is imputed to those who are saved

Easton also said, "the righteousness of Christ is imputed to them that believe in him, or so attributed to them as to be considered their own;"

The Illustrated Bible Dictionary, by M.G. Easton, Thomas Nelson, [1897]

Second Corinthians 5:21, "For he hath made him *to be* sin for us, who knew no sin; that we might be made the righteousness of God in him."

What a deal! Jesus says, "If you will give me your sin, I will give you my righteousness."

Philippians 3:9, "And be found in him, not having mine own righteousness, which is of the law, but that which is through the faith of Christ, the righteousness which is of God by faith:"

Romans 3:22, "Even the righteousness of God *which is* by faith of Jesus Christ unto all and upon all them that believe: for there is no difference:"

4. Sin will never be imputed to a believer.

God said this type of imputation will never happen.

Romans 4:7-8, "*Saying,* Blessed *are* they whose iniquities are forgiven, and whose sins are covered. Blessed *is* the man to whom the Lord will not impute sin."

Second Corinthians 5:19, "To wit, that God was

but try to keep your balance! 47

in Christ, reconciling the world unto himself, not imputing their trespasses unto them..."

As a member of Adam's race we are born in sin. The guilt of his sin is imputed to us. But then our sin is imputed to Christ as the Second Adam, so that He might pay for those sins. When we trust Christ for His forgiveness, His righteousness is imputed to us. Once God has declared us to be not guilty, sin will never again be charged (or imputed) to our account.

Our Balance Sheet **Before** *We Were Saved*

+ **Positive**	- **Negative**
No righteousness "as filthy rags"	Sins

Our Balance Sheet **After** *We Were Saved*

+ **Positive**	- **Negative**
Christ's righteousness	Justified Not guilty

God says He will never impute sin to us.

REASON #4
Because God Says the Believer Shall Never Perish

John 10:27-29, "My sheep hear my voice, and I know them, and they follow me: And I give unto them eternal life; and they shall never perish, neither shall any *man* pluck them out of my hand. My Father, which gave *them* me, is greater than all; and no *man* is able to pluck *them* out of my Father's hand."

Seven separate statements are made concerning Christ's sheep:
- My sheep.
- They hear my voice.
- I know them.
- They follow me.
- I give unto them eternal life.
- They shall never perish.
- They cannot be removed from His hand, nor His Father's hand.

The first thing we are told is that He owns the sheep. They are His because He paid for them with His own blood. Jesus said those that He gives eternal life to shall never perish. n the Greek it is more emphatic then that, it actually means "no, not ever."

John 11:21-26, "Then said Martha unto Jesus, Lord, if thou hadst been here, my brother had not

but try to keep your balance! 49

died. But I know, that even now, whatsoever thou wilt ask of God, God will give *it* thee. Jesus saith unto her, Thy brother shall rise again. Martha saith unto him, I know that he shall rise again in the resurrection at the last day. Jesus said unto her, I am the resurrection, and the life: he that believeth in me, though he were dead, yet shall he live: And whosoever liveth and believeth in me shall never die. Believest thou this?

That is a question that needs to be asked of many believers today. "Believest thou this?"

When Jesus says He gives unto us "everlasting life," believest thou this? How long does everlasting mean? When He says, "shall never die," believest thou this? What does the word "never" mean? When He says we "shall never perish," believest thou this? What does "never" mean in this verse?

When Jesus said that "whosoever liveth and believeth in me shall never die," He obviously wasn't talking about physical death. Everyone there that was alive was going to die physically. The only thing He could have been referring to was spiritual death. He promised that every believer would never die spiritually.

Hebrews 9:27, "And as it is appointed unto men once to die, but after this the judgment:" The judgment is referring to the Great White Throne Judgment.

50   TIPTOE THROUGH THE T-U-L-I-PS

John 5:24, "Verily, verily, I say unto you, He that heareth my word, and believeth on him that sent me, hath everlasting life, and shall not come into condemnation; but is passed from death unto life."

The same Greek word translated "judgment" in Hebrews 9:27, is the same word translated "condemnation" in John 5:24. Jesus said that every believer that "hath (present tense) everlasting life," "shall not come into condemnation," or judgment. Believest thou this?

When the Bible says that the believer has:
- "eternal life" (First John 5:13) "eternal salvation" (Hebrews. 5:9)
- "eternal redemption" (Hebrews. 9:12) "eternal inheritance" (Hebrews. 9:15)
- "eternal glory" (First Peter 5:10) "Believest thou this?"

When the Bible speaks of "eternal life," or "everlasting life," it always refers to this in the present tense; "have," "has," or "hath." What the believer has right now is everlasting and eternal. John 5:24 says we have "passed (past tense) from death unto life."

Colossians 1:13 says God "…hath [present tense] delivered us from the power of darkness, and hath [present tense] translated *us* into the kingdom of his dear Son:"

To see the significance of this, let's go back to the

but try to keep your balance! 51

Garden of Eden. What was the first thing Satan said to Eve? "Yea, hath God said…?" The first thing Satan did was question what God had said. Did God really mean what He said? Go through the New Testament and see all the positive statements Jesus makes about our salvation, and see if you can find the word "if" anywhere. "You have everlasting life (if) you do this, or (if) you don't do that." If we have a conditional salvation, why didn't Jesus say so? If God didn't mean what He said, why didn't He say what He meant?

REASON #5

Because God Has Predestined the Believer to Heaven

Romans chapter 8 starts out with the promise of no condemnation, and ends with the promise of no separation; in between it states that God has already glorified us. Many times in scripture God speaks of something that is to happen in the future as though it has already happened, because the outcome has already been determined and is certain.

Romans 8:29-30, "For whom he did foreknow, he also did predestinate *to be* conformed to the image of his Son, that he might be the firstborn among many brethren. Moreover whom he did predestinate, them he also called: and whom he called, them he also justified: and whom he justified, them he also glorified."

52   Tiptoe Through the T-U-L-I-Ps

According to these verses we are predestinated, called, justified, and glorified. All of these in relation to the believer are in the past tense. As far as God is concerned, we are already "glorified".

Ephesians 2:4-7, "But God, who is rich in mercy, for his great love wherewith he loved us, Even when we were dead in sins, hath quickened us together with Christ, (by grace ye are saved;) And hath raised *us* up together, and made *us* sit together in heavenly *places* in Christ Jesus: That in the ages to come he might shew the exceeding riches of his grace in *his* kindness toward us through Christ Jesus."

According to Ephesians 2:6, we are already seated with Christ in heaven positionally.

William Burkitt's Notes on the New Testament:

> The apostle here instances in two branches more of that salvation which he had in the foregoing verse affirmed to be of grace, namely, that of our resurrection and glorification; both which are yet to come, and yet they are spoken of as already past: when the Father raised and glorified Christ, all believers were raised and glorified in him; for in his resurrection and glorification he did sustain the quality of a public person, representing his whole church as their head and husband; and, accordingly, believers are and may be said to be raised already, and glorified already, not in their own persons, but in Christ their head.

CHAPTER SIX

Problem Texts Concerning the Believer's Security

(Galatians 5:4) - Falling From Grace

Many people have asked this question, "Is it possible for a Christian to backslide, and FALL FROM GRACE, and lose their salvation." There are two applications of "falling from grace" mentioned in the scripture.

Trying to mix human merit (works) and or the law with grace.

Galatians 5:1-4, "Stand fast therefore in the liberty wherewith Christ hath made us free, and be not entangled again with the yoke of bondage. [Referring here to the law] Behold, I Paul say unto you, that if ye be circumcised, Christ shall profit you nothing.

54 TIPTOE THROUGH THE T-U-L-I-PS

For I testify again to every man that is circumcised, that he is a debtor to do the whole law. Christ is become of no effect unto you, whosoever of you are justified by the law; ye are fallen from grace."

The term in the Greek here for "fallen from grace" is "ekpipto." The meaning of ekpipto is to be driven off coarse, like a ship out of control. What Paul is saying here is that you have left the sphere of grace, and have entered back into the sphere of the law. Christ had set them free from the law, but now they were trying to mix law and grace together and it doesn't work that way. You are going back under the yoke of bondage from which Christ has already set you free.

Most people who believe you can lose your salvation refer to someone as "falling from grace" if they backslide and go back into sin, but that is clearly not the case here. Actually someone who is saved that now thinks they somehow now can be justified by keeping the Law has actually "fallen from grace." They have fallen off course. Grace is what sets us free from the law.

Our lives not being a testimony of God's grace

If we are no longer under the law does that mean we can live any way we want to? Absolutely not!

Hebrews 12:14-15, "Follow peace with all *men*, and holiness, without which no man shall see the

but try to keep your balance! 55

Lord: Looking diligently lest any man **fail of the grace of God**; lest any root of bitterness springing up trouble *you*, and thereby many be defiled;"

This is the other time "ekpipto" is used. The writer of Hebrews is concerned that if a saved person is not a picture of what God's grace can do in a life, he might cause others to stumble.

Romans 5:20, "Moreover the law entered, that the offence might abound. But where sin abounded, grace did much more abound:" There is no sin that God's grace does not exceed. Does that mean we should sin more so that more of God's grace can be displayed? That is exactly what some Christians during Paul's time were saying.

Romans 3:7-8, "For if the truth of God hath more abounded through my lie unto his glory; why yet am I also judged as a sinner? And not *rather*, (as we be slanderously reported, and as some affirm that we say,) Let us do evil, that good may come? whose damnation is just."

Romans 5:20, "Moreover the law entered, that the offence might abound. But where sin abounded, grace did much more abound:"

Romans 6:1-2, "What shall we say then? Shall we continue in sin, that grace may abound? God forbid. How shall we, that are dead to sin, live any longer therein?"

How should we live because of God's grace?

Titus 2:11-14 tells us, "For the grace of God that bringeth salvation hath appeared to all men, Teaching us that, denying ungodliness and worldly lusts, we should live soberly, righteously, and godly, in this present world; Looking for that blessed hope, and the glorious appearing of the great God and our Saviour Jesus Christ; Who gave himself for us, that he might redeem us from all iniquity, and purify unto himself a peculiar people, zealous of good works."

The believer is to live in such a way as to be a testimony of what the grace of God can do in a life.

Does sin in a Christian's life ever bring glory to God? Of course not! This is the main difference between law and grace. The law can't change a person on the inside or give them new life, only the grace of God can. That is the way we are to live before a lost world. If I don't live that way, do these verses say I will no longer be saved? Absolutely not!

Falling from grace is never used in relation to a believer losing their salvation, that is a misinterpretation of those verses. Those who teach that a person can lose their salvation have actually "fallen from grace." They have left the sphere of grace and have entered back into the sphere of works. They do not have a clear understanding of what grace means, nor of the meaning of these verses.

but try to keep your balance!

(HEBREWS 6:4-6) THE UNPARDONABLE SIN

Hebrews 6:4-6, "For *it is* impossible for those who were once enlightened, and have tasted of the heavenly gift, and were made partakers of the Holy Ghost, And have tasted the good word of God, and the powers of the world to come, If they shall fall away, to renew them again unto repentance; seeing they crucify to themselves the Son of God afresh, and put *him* to an open shame."

There are at least four different interpretations of this passage.

- This is referring to an unsaved Hebrew, who is convinced of the truth of Jesus being the Messiah, but rejects it and returns to Judaism. Compare with Matthew 12:31-32. If an unsaved Jew rejected Jesus as the Messiah, this would be the blasphemy of the Holy Spirit, and the only sin he could not be forgiven for.
- This is a saved person that is backslidden, and while in this backslidden condition is putting Christ to an open shame, and cannot be brought back to repentance while in this condition.
- This is saying that it is impossible for a saved person to ever be lost again, and then go back and be saved a second time.

58 TIPTOE THROUGH THE T-U-L-I-PS

- This is a saved person that renounces Christianity, turns against Christ, and openly apostatizes from his religion, and falls from grace and is lost. If they do this they will perish, because they renounce the only way of salvation, and treat Christ as an imposter, deserving of crucifixion.

Although I hold to #3, only the last interpretation presents any real problems. If the last were true, it would seem to indicate that if a saved person backslides, they would be hopelessly lost and cannot be renewed again to salvation.

The writer of Hebrews goes on to say in verses 9 and 10, "But, beloved, we are persuaded better things of you, and things that accompany salvation, though we thus speak. For God *is* not unrighteous to forget your work and labour of love, which ye have shewed toward his name, in that ye have ministered to the saints, and do minister."

Hebrews 6:18-20, "That by two immutable things, in which *it was* impossible for God to lie, we might have a strong consolation, who have fled for refuge to lay hold upon the hope set before us: Which *hope* we have as an anchor of the soul, both sure and stedfast, and which entereth into that within the veil; Whither the forerunner is for us entered, *even* Jesus, made an high priest for ever after the or-

but try to keep your balance! 59

der of Melchisedec."

These verses are assurances of the believer's security in Christ, because it is based upon God's promises.

This passage certainly cannot be referring to a believer who has fallen into sin.

(SECOND PETER 2:20-22) DOGS AND SOWS

Second Peter 2:20-22, "For if after they have escaped the pollutions of the world through the knowledge of the Lord and Saviour Jesus Christ, they are again entangled therein, and overcome, the latter end is worse with them than the beginning. For it had been better for them not to have known the way of righteousness, than, after they have known *it*, to turn from the holy commandment delivered unto them But it is happened unto them according to the true proverb, The dog *is* turned to his own vomit again; and the sow that was washed to her wallowing in the mire."

Some people believe these verses are talking about a saved person that becomes entangled again in sin, and finally is lost. However, God never refers to His people as dogs or pigs. Verse 22 indicates that a dog is still a dog, and a hog is still a hog. Some people get changed on the outside, but their inner nature is not changed, because they have never been

60   TIPTOE THROUGH THE T-U-L-I-PS

born again.

God is referring here to enlightened lost people who return to their sins and do not accept Christ.

Matthew 12:43-45, "When the unclean spirit is gone out of a man, he walketh through dry places, seeking rest, and findeth none. Then he saith, I will return into my house from whence I came out; and when he is come, he findeth *it* empty, swept, and garnished. Then goeth he, and taketh with himself seven other spirits more wicked than himself, and they enter in and dwell there: and the last *state* of that man is worse than the first. Even so shall it be also unto this wicked generation."

This is another passage that deals with a person that has cleaned themselves up, but has not received Christ into their heart to dwell there.

(EZEKIEL 3:20-21) RIGHTEOUS MAN TURNS FROM RIGHTEOUSNESS

Does this passage teach that if a Christian backslides they can lose their soul?

Ezekiel 3:20-21, "Again, When a righteous *man* doth turn from his righteousness, and commit iniquity, and I lay a stumblingblock before him, he shall die: because thou hast not given him warning, he shall die in his sin, and his righteousness which he hath done shall not be remembered; but his blood will I require at thine hand. Nevertheless if thou

but try to keep your balance! 61

warn the righteous *man*, that the righteous sin not, and he doth not sin, he shall surely live, because he is warned; also thou hast delivered thy soul."

This passage is not talking about the salvation of a soul, or the loss of a soul. This has to do with a citizen of Israel keeping the Mosaiac Law. The penalty is not the loss of a soul, but physical death.

See also Ezekiel 18:24 and Ezekiel 33:12-13 which are nearly identical.

(EXODUS 32:31-33) NAMES BLOTTED OUT OF HIS BOOK (REVELATION 3:5)

Can a saved person have their name blotted out of the Book of Life and be lost?

Exodus 32:31-33, "And Moses returned unto the LORD, and said, Oh, this people have sinned a great sin, and have made them gods of gold. Yet now, if thou wilt forgive their sin—; and if not, blot me, I pray thee, out of thy book which thou hast written. And the LORD said unto Moses, Whosoever hath sinned against me, him will I blot out of my book."

Revelation 3:5, "He that overcometh, the same shall be clothed in white raiment; and I will not blot out his name out of the book of life, but I will confess his name before my Father, and before his angels."

There are several possibilities:

- Our names are written in the Book of Life

when we are saved, and can be blotted out later, thus a saved person can be lost.
- All our names are written in the Book of Life when we are born, then those who reject Christ are blotted out later and removed.
- Revelation 3:5 is just an assurance to the believer that God will never remove their name from the Book of Life.
- Exodus 32 may not be talking about the Book of Life at all, but another book.

Please realize that the believer is never told that their name will ever be blotted out at all, they are just assured that it won't be.

(First Corinthians 9:27) Lest I Should Be A Castaway

Does this scripture teach that a saved person can be lost?

First Corinthians 9:27, "But I keep under my body, and bring *it* into subjection: lest that by any means, when I have preached to others, I myself should be a castaway."

The word "castaway" is from a Greek word that means "not approved." Paul was concerned that he would keep his natural desires under control so that he would not become unprofitable for the Lord's

but try to keep your balance! 63

work, and thus lose his ministry. This has happened to many that were once in the ministry. Paul was not afraid of losing his salvation, just his opportunity to minister in the field God had called him to.

In First Corinthians chapter 6, Paul lists the different ways a man can break the law, verses 9-10, "Know ye not that the unrighteous shall not inherit the kingdom of God? Be not deceived: neither fornicators, nor idolaters, nor adulterers, nor effeminate, nor abusers of themselves with mankind, Nor thieves, nor covetous, nor drunkards, nor revilers, nor extortioners, shall inherit the kingdom of God."

Now notice what he says in verses 11-12, "And such were some of you: but ye are washed, but ye are sanctified, but ye are justified in the name of the Lord Jesus, and by the Spirit of our God. All things are lawful unto me, but all things are not expedient: all things are lawful for me, but I will not be brought under the power of any."

In verse 12 Paul makes an amazing statement. After listing the ways a man can break the law, he says all things are lawful unto him. Was Paul saying it was all right for him to do those things? Of course not. However, Paul understood he was no longer under the law. But many things that might be considered lawful, would not be "expedient" for him to do. Expedient means "the means to an end." Paul

64   Tiptoe Through the T-U-L-I-Ps

also said he was not going to be brought under the power of anything, even if it were considered lawful. But Paul did not fear it would cause him to lose his salvation.

Just because we are secure, never gives us a license to sin.

Romans 11:22

"Behold therefore the goodness and severity of God: on them which fell, severity; but toward thee, goodness, **if thou continue** in *his* goodness: otherwise thou also shalt be **cut off**."

If we go back to the beginning of the chapter, the question is asked: "Hath God cast away his people?" And Paul says: "God forbid." He then adds: "God hath not cast away his people which he foreknew." When Paul speaks of God's foreknowledge of Israel, it is the same word used in Romans 8:29 concerning His foreknowledge of the church. Keep in mind when His foreknowledge of either one is discussed it refers more to corporate Israel and the church, rather than to individuals. God chose out a plan to choose out a people.

In verses 2-4 it speaks of Elijah thinking he was all alone, but God said He had a remnant that had not bowed the knee to Baal. Then in verses 5 & 6 it says this: "Even so then at this present time also there is a remnant according to the election of grace.

but try to keep your balance! 65

And if by grace, then *is it* no more of works: otherwise grace is no more grace. But if *it be* of works, then is it no more grace: otherwise work is no more work."

There are two things we need to be clear on in this passage: God will not cast away His elect whom He foreknew, and we are saved by grace, not by works. Everything else in this passage should be interpreted in that light.

Verses 7 thru 11 speak of Israel's blindness corporately, which allowed God to offer salvation by grace unto the Gentiles. Verses 11-14 also speak of Paul's desire for Israel to be jealous because of God turning now to the Gentiles, so that possibly at least some of them could be saved. So when it says "cast away," it is referring to God's turning away from Israel, to His turning now to the Gentiles. This casting away is not referring to individuals, but of Israel corporately. The word for "casting away" also carries more a meaning of loss, than of rejection.

Please remember, the remnant of Israel that was saved (see also Romans 9:27), was saved by grace, not by their works, according to verse 5 & 6.

In verses 15 thru 24 it points out the fact that the branches which were broken off were because of unbelief. This is representative of unbelieving Israel. But those that did not continue in unbelief, would be grafted in.

I believe the idea in verse 22 about continuing

66   Tiptoe Through the T-U-L-I-Ps

in His goodness is not a prescription for maintaining our position in Christ by good works, or that we could lose that position of being His elect; but is rather dealing with God's blessing in relation to chastening. Through disobedience we risk being cut off from God's blessing. I believe this interpretation would be consistent with the rest of this passage.

Colossians 1:23

"**If** ye continue in the faith grounded and settled, and *be* **not moved away** from the hope of the gospel, which ye have heard, *and* which was preached to every creature which is under heaven; whereof I Paul am made a minister;"

In First Peter 1:2, 4-5 it says the "Elect according to the foreknowledge of God the Father... an inheritance incorruptible, and undefiled, and that fadeth not away, reserved in heaven for you, Who are kept by the power of God through faith unto salvation ready to be revealed in the last time."

We have an inheritance that nothing can have an affect on that is reserved for us, and we do not keep ourselves, but we are kept by the power of God. In Colossians 1:5 it says we have a "...hope which is laid up for you in heaven, whereof ye heard before in the word of the truth of the gospel;" In verses 13 and 14 it says that God "...hath delivered us from the power of darkness, and hath translated *us* into

but try to keep your balance! 67

the kingdom of his dear Son: In whom we have redemption through his blood, *even* the forgiveness of sins:" We have been translated from the power of darkness into the kingdom of His dear Son. We are in His kingdom now.

In verses 10 and 11 it says that Paul's desire for the believers at Colosse was "That ye might walk worthy of the Lord unto all pleasing, being fruitful in every good work, and increasing in the knowledge of God; Strengthened with all might, according to his glorious power, unto all patience and longsuffering with joyfulness;"

In verse 20, in reference to Christ, it says: "And, having made peace through the blood of his cross, by him to reconcile all things unto himself…" and it continues in verse 22 "…to present you holy and unblameable and unreproveable in his sight:" When we stand before the Judgment Seat of Christ, will we all be "unblameable" and "unreproveable"? Clearly not. Wouldn't it be great if every one of us continued "in the faith grounded and settled," and were not "moved away from the hope of the gospel," in any way? When we stand before Him in that judgment though, do we still have that inheritance reserved for us? Of course we do. Is there anything there that suggests we have lost our inheritance, or that God has been unable to keep us, or we will be kicked out of His kingdom? No.

HEBREWS 3:6 AND 3:14

"But Christ as a son over his own house; whose house are we, if we hold fast the confidence and the rejoicing of the hope firm **unto the end**."

"For we are made partakers of Christ, **if we hold the beginning of our confidence stedfast unto the end;**"

The book of Hebrews is of course a transitional book moving from the Old Testament system into the church age. Chapters three and four are dealing with those in Israel who had not entered into God's rest because of unbelief. But Hebrews 4:1-2 says, "Let us therefore fear, lest, a promise being left *us* of entering into his rest, any of you should seem to come short of it. For unto us was the gospel preached, as well as unto them: but the word preached did not profit them, not being mixed with faith in them that heard *it*." They heard the gospel, but it did not profit them because it was not mixed with faith.

In Hebrews 4:3 it clearly states: "For we which have believed do enter into rest…" and it goes on to say in verse 6, "…they to whom it was first preached entered not in because of unbelief:" If those that believed the gospel have entered into God's rest, then what does it mean in 3:6 and 3:14 about "…if we hold fast the confidence…" and "…if we hold the beginning of our confidence stedfast unto the

but try to keep your balance! 69

end…"? Hebrews 3:10 says those that had not entered into God's rest "…have not known my ways." What does it mean then to "…hold fast the beginning of our confidence unto the end…"? Who is it that is made a partaker of Christ, and enters into God's rest? Those that have exercised faith, and believed to the saving of their soul.

There was a man that once attended Trinity Baptist Church for a number of years. Came to the services, sang the songs, but was never saved, nor is he saved today. He never became a partaker of Christ, nor did he enter into God's rest for the believer. Could it be said that he did not hold fast his confidence unto the end? Remember, it is God that keeps us, not we ourselves. Anyone that believes we must hold out unto the end to be saved does not have a proper understanding of the grace of God as pertaining to our salvation.

SECOND PETER 1:10-11

"Wherefore the rather, brethren, give diligence to make your calling and election sure: for if ye do these things, **ye shall never fall**: For so an entrance shall be ministered unto you abundantly into the everlasting kingdom of our Lord and Saviour Jesus Christ."

Here again we need to go back to the verses preceding these two verses to discern the context.

70   Tiptoe Through the T-U-L-I-Ps

In verse 1 we find it is addressed to "…them that have obtained like precious faith with us through the righteousness of God and our Saviour Jesus Christ:" Verses 3 and 4 say, "According as his divine power hath given unto us all things that *pertain* unto life and godliness, through the knowledge of him that hath called us to glory and virtue: Whereby are given unto us exceeding great and precious promises: that by these ye might be partakers of the divine nature, having escaped the corruption that is in the world through lust."

Now verses 5 through 7 say: "And beside this, giving all diligence, add to your faith virtue; and to virtue knowledge; And to knowledge temperance; and to temperance patience; and to patience godliness; And to godliness brotherly kindness; and to brotherly kindness charity." Through all of these things we are growing in Christ, and becoming more like Him.

Look what verse 8 says will be the result of that: "For if these things be in you, and abound, they make *you that ye shall* neither *be* barren nor unfruitful in the knowledge of our Lord Jesus Christ."

Verse 9 tells us what the result will be if we don't grow in this manner: "But he that lacketh these things is blind, and cannot see afar off, and hath forgotten that he was purged from his old sins." Just the opposite of verse 8, we will be barren and unfruit-

but try to keep your balance! 71

ful.

Now verses 10 and 11 say, "Wherefore the rather, brethren, give diligence to make your calling and election sure: for if ye do these things, ye shall never fall: For so an entrance shall be ministered unto you abundantly into the everlasting kingdom of our Lord and Saviour Jesus Christ." The term for "fall" is to stumble or be tripped up. It doesn't mean "lost". It also doesn't indicate they won't enter into the kingdom. It just refers to the type of entrance they will have. In verse 10 when it says "...give diligence to make your calling and election sure..." the word "sure" or "bebaios," means stable or firm. It definitely doesn't give any kind of indication that a saved person can be lost.

FIRST JOHN 2:24

"Let that therefore abide in you, which ye have heard from the beginning. If that which ye have heard from the beginning shall remain in you, ye also shall continue in the Son, and in the Father."

What does it mean that if they let that which they heard from the beginning remain in them, they would "...continue in the Son, and in the Father"? These believers were being seduced (see v. 26) by certain "antichrists" that were denying that Jesus was the Christ. John said these antichrists went out from them, because they were not of them, or else

"...they would no doubt have continued with us." John said if you deny the Son, you don't have the Father either.

This passage is just a contrast between believing the truth and continuing on, or denying the truth and going out from them and not continuing on. It has nothing to do with a saved person losing their salvation.

REVELATION 2:7 AND REVELATION 2:11

"He that hath an ear, let him hear what the Spirit saith unto the churches; To him that overcometh will I give to eat of the tree of life, which is in the midst of the paradise of God."

"He that hath an ear, let him hear what the Spirit saith unto the churches; He that overcometh shall not be hurt of the second death."

His message to each of the seven churches concludes with certain promises to those who are overcomers. The word actually means to conquer. They are promised the right to partake of the tree of life in heaven, they will not be hurt of the second death, etc. He concludes in chapter three with this: "Behold, I stand at the door, and knock: if any man hear my voice, and open the door, I will come in to him, and will sup with him, and he with me. To him that overcometh will I grant to sit with me in my throne,

but try to keep your balance! 73

even as I also overcame, and am set down with my Father in his throne. He that hath an ear, let him hear what the Spirit saith unto the churches." (Revelation 3:20-22) When we respond to His voice, and let Him in, He will come in, sup with us, and we with Him.

All of these promises are given to those who overcome. How do we overcome? Is it through our own efforts? First Corinthians 15:57 says: "But thanks *be* to God, which giveth us the victory through our Lord Jesus Christ." First John 5:4 says: "For whatsoever is born of God overcometh the world: and this is the victory that overcometh the world, *even* our faith." We are overcomers through the new birth, by placing our faith in the Lord Jesus Christ, Who gives us the victory. None of these verses have anything to do with a saved person losing their salvation.

VERSES OF COMFORT AND ASSURANCE:

Romans 5:8-10, "But God commendeth his love toward us, in that, while we were yet sinners, Christ died for us. Much more then, being now justified by his blood, we shall be saved from wrath through him. For if, when we were enemies, we were reconciled to God by the death of his Son, much more, being reconciled, we shall be saved by his life."

First Peter 1:3-5, "Blessed *be* the God and Fa-

74 TIPTOE THROUGH THE T-U-L-I-PS

ther of our Lord Jesus Christ, which according to his abundant mercy hath begotten us again unto a lively hope by the resurrection of Jesus Christ from the dead, To an inheritance incorruptible, and undefiled, and that fadeth not away, reserved in heaven for you, Who are kept by the power of God through faith unto salvation ready to be revealed in the last time."

Second Timothy 1:12, "For the which cause I also suffer these things: nevertheless I am not ashamed: for I know whom I have believed, and am persuaded that he is able to keep that which I have committed unto him against that day."

Philippians 1:6, "Being confident of this very thing, that he which hath begun a good work in you will perform *it* until the day of Jesus Christ:"

Romans 8:38-39, "For I am persuaded, that neither death, nor life, nor angels, nor principalities, nor powers, nor things present, nor things to come, Nor height, nor depth, nor any other creature, shall be able to separate us from the love of God, which is in Christ Jesus our Lord."

Hebrews 13:5, "*Let your* conversation *be* without covetousness; *and be* content with such things as ye have: for he hath said, I will never leave thee, nor forsake thee."

Jude 24, "Now unto him that is able to keep you from falling, and to present *you* faultless before the presence of his glory with exceeding joy,"

PART TWO
Calvinism

CHAPTER SEVEN

The Five Points of Calvinism

After we left the Holiness Movement, a friend of mine loaned me a book to read by a five-point Calvinist. My former pastor had talked about Calvinists, so I was eager to see what they had to say.

As I began to read this book, once again I kept coming across statements that I could not accept as being scriptural. I had just come from a church that placed great emphasis on the free will of man, and little on God's Sovereignty. Now I was reading a book by someone who placed great emphasis upon God's Sovereignty, and little if any at all on man's free will. Yet, both of these truths are clearly taught in the Bible. Shouldn't there be a balance somewhere?

Here are the "Five Points of Calvinism," also referred to as the T-U-L-I-P theory, some may word the definitions somewhat differently:

Total Depravity
A lost sinner cannot repent, cannot believe, unless he is foreordained to repent and unless God overpowers him, and God has chosen not to overpower many.

Unconditional Election
People are elected to be saved without any reference to anything they may do, and people are foreordained to be damned, unconditionally.

Limited Atonement
Christ really died only for those who are ordained to be saved. He did not atone for the sins of those He foreordained to be lost.

Irresistible Grace
It is foolish to urge people to decide, because those who are ordained to be saved will be irresistibly moved and overpowered by God's grace, and so will be saved.

Perseverance of the Saints
God will give the elect the ability to persevere.

but try to keep your balance! 79

To my knowledge, the Arminian churches do not have their own T-U-L-I-P theory as such. However, if they did, it would resemble something like this:

Total Human Ability, or Free Will
Everyone has the ability to accept or reject God's offer of salvation. Man can choose good or evil in spiritual matters.

Universal Redemption, or General Atonement
Although Christ died for all men, only those who choose to believe on Him are saved.

Limited Atonement
Man's free will limits the application of Christ's saving work. The Holy Spirit cannot regenerate anyone until they believe.

Individual Resistance
Because man is free to choose, he can resist the Holy Spirit's call. Man's election is conditioned upon what man will do, before and after salvation.

Perseverance By the Saints
Those who believe and are saved, can lose their salvation and fall from grace, if they do not keep up their faith and persevere to the end.

Here is another T-U-L-I-P theory, one that I believe is from a more balanced Biblical perspective:

Total Unworthiness

There is nothing within man, nor is there any good work that man may do, that could in any way merit him eternal life. Salvation is offered to us completely on the basis of God's grace.

Unconditional Love

God's love for us is not based on how good we are, but is in spite of how bad we can be.

Limited Atonement

Jesus died once for all.

Individual Responsibility

Man, as a free moral agent, is at liberty to act according to his choice, without compulsion or restraint, and is personally responsible to God for his choices. Each of us must choose to either accept Jesus Christ as our Lord and Saviour, or to reject Him and be lost.

Preservation of the Saviour

Once we accept Christ and trust Him to save us, we belong to Him for all eternity. Jesus Christ will keep those that belong to Him, and it is His keeping

but try to keep your balance! 81

power that guarantees our eternal salvation, not our own efforts.

If you are going to tiptoe through the T-U-L-I-Ps please try to keep your balance!

CHAPTER EIGHT

Ten Scriptural Errors Of Calvinism

I. What is a Calvinist?

A Calvinist is someone who believes in one or more of the main teachings of John Calvin. John Calvin was a French theologian and religious reformer who lived in Switzerland in the 1500s (1509-1564).

II. How was Calvin deceived?

Second Corinthians 11:3-4, "But I fear, lest by any means, as the serpent beguiled Eve through his **subtilty**, so your minds should be corrupted from the **simplicity** that is in Christ. For if **he that cometh** preacheth **another Jesus**, whom we have not preached, or *if* ye receive **another spirit**, which ye have not received, or **another gospel**, which ye

have not accepted, **ye might well bear with *him*.**"
Or in other words, Paul was saying, "I'm afraid you
might believe them."

Another Jesus, another spirit, another gospel; as
Dr. Mickey Carter has pointed out, "Things that are
different are not the same."

What the Apostle Paul was afraid of for the
Corinthian believers has happened many times in
the last 2000 years. Satan deceives one person into
thinking they have been given spiritual insight that
nobody else has ("your eyes shall be opened" Gene-
sis.3:5), and they ("he that cometh") end up preaching "another Jesus (attacks His person and work),"
"another spirit (attacks His person and work)," and
"another gospel (God's method of salvation)."

III. The Ten Errors

The 5 main beliefs of Calvinism are called the T-
U-L-I-P theory. Like evolution, it is not a fact.

1. TOTAL DEPRAVITY
The error:

When Calvinists say "total depravity," they actually mean "total inability."

A lost sinner cannot repent, cannot believe, unless he is foreordained to repent and unless God
overpowers him, and God has chosen not to overpower many.

but try to keep your balance! 85

(Why then does God command us to go into all the world and preach the gospel to **every** creature, if **all** cannot respond?)

In practice, Calvinists believe man does not really have a free will. (This eliminates man's personal responsibility. If man does not have a free will, how can he be guilty when he does wrong? It also is an attack against the work of the Holy Spirit, and helps to introduce another gospel.)

The scriptural response:

In John 16:7-12 it speaks of the function of the Holy Spirit when He was to come. Verse 8 says He would, "...reprove the world of sin, and of righteousness, and of judgment:" The word "reprove" is "elegho" which means to admonish, convict, convince, tell a fault. The word for world "kosmos," means the world and its inhabitants.

In verse 9 Jesus points out the Holy Spirit would convict the world of sin, because they believe not on Him. It was the sin of unbelief for which they would be convicted. How could the Holy Spirit convince them of their unbelief if they had no power to believe or couldn't understand?

Man was created with these three qualities: reason, conscience and will.

Reason is the mind's power of drawing conclusions and determining truth. *Conscience* is the consciousness of our own acts and feelings as right or wrong. *Will* is the faculty for making choices and the act of using this power. (Man's volition.) Man, as a free moral agent, is at liberty to act according to his choice, without compulsion or restraint, but is personally responsible to God for his choices.

The only thing man is asked to do in salvation is believe. The only sin that God holds man responsible for is unbelief. Would God ask man to do something he couldn't, then hold him responsible because he didn't? God is not an unjust God. He is a righteous judge.

If a lost person cannot understand and believe the gospel, Second Corinthians 4:3-4 makes no sense at all. "But if our gospel be hid, it is hid to them that are lost: In whom the god of this world [Satan] hath blinded the minds of them which believe not, lest the light of the glorious gospel of Christ, who is the image of God, should shine unto them."

According to God's Word, Satan is actively blinding peoples' minds so they can't understand the gospel. That wouldn't be necessary if the lost couldn't understand anyway. Satan is active in trying to blind the minds of saved people too through false doctrine.

but try to keep your balance!

2. UNCONDITIONAL ELECTION
The error:

People are elected to be saved without any reference to anything they may do, and people are foreordained to be damned, unconditionally.

(This is a teaching contrary to the "simplicity" of the gospel message. This is also fatalism, and makes preaching the gospel seem foolish and undermines evangelism in the church. It also is an attack on the character of God.)

The scriptural response:

Does God ever choose someone because of something that God saw in them? Why did God choose Abraham to be the father of a great and mighty nation, in whom all the nations of the earth would be blessed? In Genesis 18:17-19 it says, "And the LORD said... Abraham shall surely become a great and mighty nation, and all the nations of the earth shall be blessed in him... **For I know him,** that **he will** command his children and his household after him, and **they shall** keep the way of the LORD, to do justice and judgment; that the LORD **may** bring upon Abraham that which he hath spoken of him." God chose Abraham because of His foreknowledge, and what He saw in him.

In Genesis 22:16-18, God asked Abraham to sacrifice his only son, even though God had already promised that through this child He was going to bless all nations. v. 16, "...By myself have I sworn, saith the LORD, for **because** thou hast done this thing, and hast not withheld thy son, thine only *son*..." v. 17, "That in blessing I will bless thee..." v. 18, "And in thy seed shall all nations of the earth be blessed; **because thou hast obeyed my voice.**" See Genesis 26:3-5 also. God chose Abraham and promised His blessing on him because He foreknew the choice Abraham would make.

God does not damn anyone unconditionally. Second Thessalonians 2:8-14 indicates it is because of an act of the **will** that an unbeliever is damned. The unbelievers "...**received not** the love of the truth, that they **might** be saved." To **receive** something takes an act of the **will**. The unbeliever makes himself "a vessel of wrath, fitted for destruction," through his own choice.

Although God does not choose or damn anyone unconditionally, God does love unconditionally. His love for us is not based on how good we are, but is in spite of how bad we can be.

3. LIMITED ATONEMENT
The error:

Christ really died only for those who are ordained to be saved; He did not atone for the sins of those He foreordained to be lost. God does not love the

but try to keep your balance!

whole world, just His elect. (Calvin placed a limit on Christ's atonement that God didn't put there in His Word. Calvinists show God as having compassion on some but not on others. This is a clear attack on the work of Christ, and the character of God. Satan likes to try to bring God down to man's level.)

The scriptural response:

John 3:16-17, "For God so loved **the world** that he gave his only begotten son, that **whosoever** believeth in him, shall not perish but have everlasting life." That is not just the elect.

Verse 17 says, "For God sent not his son into **the world** to condemn the world; but that **the world** through him **might** be saved." The Bible says that God not only loves **the whole world**, but Christ's death made it possible that the whole world **might** be saved. If God didn't mean what He said, why didn't He say what He meant?

First John 2:1-2, "My little children, these things write I unto you, that ye sin not. And if any man sin we have an advocate with the Father, Jesus Christ the righteous: And he is the **propitiation for our sins**; and not for ours only, but **also for *the sins of the whole world.***" (Not just the elect!) Whenever scripture contradicts their teaching, Calvinists attempt to explain the verses away.

First Timothy 2:3-4, "For this *is* good and acceptable in the sight of God our Saviour; Who will have **all men to be saved**, and to come unto the knowledge of the truth." Calvinists say "all men" means just the elect.

Second Peter 3:9, "The Lord is not slack concerning his promise; as some men count slackness; but is longsuffering to us-ward, **not willing that any should perish**, but that **all should come to repentance**." Calvinists say "any" and "all" are just the elect.

There are many parallels between a belief in Calvinism, and a belief in the theory of evolution. For example: All known scientific evidences fit the creation model. There are multiplied thousands of evidences that do not fit the evolution model. The creation model can **predict** these scientific evidences; but they have to be **explained** so as to fit the evolution model. If something just can't be explained, the evolutionist just says, "Although we can't explain how it fits right now, we know we will be able to someday." This is the same reply the Calvinist gives.

Many verses talk about God loving the whole world, and Christ dying for the whole world etc., which would be predicted by a balanced view of salvation; but the Calvinists have to try to make these verses mean just the elect. Many other such examples could be given.

but try to keep your balance! 91

4. Irresistible Grace

The error:

It is foolish to urge people to decide, because those who are ordained to be saved will irresistibly be moved and overpowered by God's grace, and so will be saved.

They basically use two verses for this:

- John 6:44, "No man can come to me, except the Father which hath sent me draw him."
- Matthew 22:14, "For many are called, but few are chosen."

The scriptural response:

John 6:45 says, "It is written in the prophets, And they shall be **all** taught of God…" The **all** must not be overlooked. In verse 51 Jesus said, "I am the living bread…If **any man** eat of this bread, he shall live forever…" The verse concludes, "…my flesh, which I will give for the life of **the world."**

Verse 44 is preceded by verse 40, the last words in each of which are identical. Verse 40 says, "…this is the will of him that sent me, that every one which seeth the Son, and believeth on him, **may** have everlasting life…" Seeing and believing precedes the statement of the drawing.

In John 5:40 Jesus said, "And ye will not come to me, that ye might have life." This was man's fault and he is responsible for his choice.

In John 12:32 Jesus said, "And I, if I be lifted up from the earth, will draw **all** *men* unto me." All are drawn, but not all respond.

In response to Matthew 22:14, "For many are called, but few *are* chosen."

"Called" being distinguished from "chosen," it can only mean invited. The "chosen" are those who put on the wedding garment provided by the King. Many were invited, but few accepted the invitation.

Romans 1:16, "For I am not ashamed of the gospel of Christ: for it is the power of God unto salvation to every one that believeth; to the Jew first, and also to the Greek."

The Calvinist believes irresistible grace is the power that produces salvation. The Bible says the gospel of Christ is the power of God unto salvation.

5. Perseverance of the Saints

The error:

God will give the elect the ability to persevere. (This is an attack upon the keeping power of Christ. We don't have to persevere; we are kept.)

The scriptural response:

Philippians 1:6, "Being confident of this very thing, that he which hath begun a good work in you

but try to keep your balance! 93

will perform *it* until the day of Jesus Christ." See also John 6:40.

First Peter 1:5, "Who are kept by the power of God through faith unto salvation ready to be revealed in the last time."

It is not the "Perseverance of the Saints," but the "Preservation of the Saviour." Once we accept Christ and trust Him to save us, we belong to Him for all eternity. Jesus Christ will keep those that belong to Him, and it is His keeping power that guarantees our eternal salvation, not our own efforts.

6. BELIEVING IS A WORK
The error:

Calvinism says that if a person can accept or reject salvation, this would make him in control of his destiny and not God. They say believing and trusting is a work. (This eliminates man's free will and accountability and makes God someone we can't trust; God just makes it appear that man must choose. It also is once again a clear contradiction of scripture)

The scriptural response:

In Romans 4:2-5, Abraham just believed what God said, and trusted Him to do what He said He would. This chapter clearly teaches that Abraham didn't do any work, he just believed God. But yet it

94   Tiptoe Through the T-U-L-I-Ps

was his exercise of faith that justified him. However, God's Word says believing and trusting are the opposite of works. That is how God looks at it. "Yea, hath God said…?"

Dr. Griffith Thomas said, "There is no credit or merit in the act of believing, for trust in another is absolutely incompatible with self-righteousness and dependence on our own powers. …Faith is the condition, not the ground of salvation." (Epistle to Romans, Vol. 1, pp. 154, 165)

7. Faith is a Gift

The error:

Because a lost person is spiritually dead, he will not respond to spiritual truth, therefore God must give him the gift of faith before he can believe. (This is charging God with telling man to do something he actually can't do.)

The scriptural response:

Calvinists believe that faith is a gift because of a misunderstanding of Ephesians 2:8-9.

They teach "faith" is the gift of God and not salvation by grace through faith. "For by grace are ye saved through faith; and that not of yourselves: *it is* the gift of God: Not of works, lest any man should boast."

If we were to diagram verse 8 in the English

but try to keep your balance! 95

language: "ye" is the noun; "saved" is the verb; "by grace" and "through faith" are prepositional phrases that modify the verb "saved." These words describe our salvation.

The Greek word for "that" in verse 8 is neuter, so that the reference cannot be to "faith," since in that case it would be feminine. The two clauses, "not of yourselves and "not of works" must of necessity refer to the same thing. Romans 6:23 says, "...the gift of God *is* eternal life through Jesus Christ our Lord."

The demonstrative pronoun "that" (touto), which is neuter in verse 8, refers to the preceding clause or phrase in its entirety but cannot refer to the words "grace", "faith", or "saved" individually. Thus the word "that" would refer to the concept of salvation whose basis is by grace through faith. One could view Ephesians 2:8 as follows: "and this salvation (which comes by grace through faith) is not of yourselves, it is a gift from God; this salvation is not a result of works, that no one should boast."

Hebrews 11:1 defines "faith" as "...the substance of things hoped for, the evidence of things not seen." If you can see it or hold it in your hand that doesn't take any faith on your part. Faith as described in Hebrews 11 is not described as an infused or transmitted substance, but as a human response. .

Samuel Fisk said, "It is true in one sense that

faith is the gift of God, but it is God's gift to all who want it, to all who are willing to use it. Since, as is most generally agreed, the sincere offer of salvation is made to all, and since "whosoever will" may receive the gospel, it is evident that saving faith is within the reach of all.

Such faith is given of God to those who desire to be saved. It is not given to all, because all will not avail themselves of it, will not yield to the moving of the Holy Spirit, and will not let the regenerating power of God work within them.

Dr. R.A. Torrey said, "Faith is God's gift. Like all of God's gifts it is at the disposal of all who wish it, for there is no respect of persons with Him."

Dr. Harry Ironside said, "All men have faith if they will; but alas, many refuse to hear the Word of God, so they are left in their unbelief. (Faith is God's gift) because it is given through His Word."

Faith as used in the New Testament (Strong's Concordance):

- "elpis" = confidence. Only used once in N.T., Hebrews 10:23, "…hold fast the profession of your faith."
- "oligopistos" = lacking confidence. Only used 5 times in the N.T. Ex.: Matthew 6:30, "O ye of little faith."
- "pistis" = Persuasion, conviction of truth, to rely upon, faithfulness, the system of

but try to keep your balance! 97

religious faith, assurance, belief, fidelity. This is the word most often used and it can have many meanings.

Our English dictionary gives these meanings to faith:
- A confident belief in the truth, or trustworthiness of a person, idea, or thing.
- Belief that does not rest on logical proof or material evidence.
- Loyalty to a person or thing.
- Belief and trust in God and in the scriptures. Religious conviction.
- A system of religious beliefs.
- Any set of principles or beliefs.

Faith is always seen as a human response to someone, or to a set of beliefs; or the set of beliefs themselves. Faith is never something transmitted to someone.

8. FAITH COMES BEFORE HEARING
The error:

A lost person cannot understand spiritual truths. Therefore, God has to give a lost person the gift of faith first, and then only will he understand what he hears. (The simple gospel message says, "Trust and obey," while the Calvinists say, "They really can't

98 TIPTOE THROUGH THE T-U-L-I-Ps

and won't," unless God does something else first. It also takes away from the work of the Holy Spirit in convincing the lost for the sin of unbelief.)

The scriptural response:
Romans 10:9-17

Verse 14 says, "How then shall they call on him in whom they have not believed? and how shall they believe in him of whom they have not heard?..." It goes on to say in verse 17: "...faith *cometh* by hearing, and hearing by the word of God." In this passage, does faith come first, or hearing the word of God? This passage asks the question, how can anyone believe without hearing about Christ first? The Bible says that hearing the word of God is what produces faith, but Calvinism teaches that God gives you faith, and then you hear the word and respond. Should I believe the Calvinist or God's Word?

9. THE NEW BIRTH COMES BEFORE HEARING

The error:
They teach that the Holy Spirit regenerates and gives new life to a lost sinner before he hears and believes the gospel. (This is an attack on the gospel message, and the work of the Holy Spirit, and questions the Word of God.)

"Yea hath God said...?"

but try to keep your balance! 99

The spiritual response:

John 20:31, "But these are written [1. the Word of God is listed first], that ye might believe [2. believing comes next] that Jesus is the Christ, the Son of God; and that believing ye might have life [3. eternal life is received last] through his name." That order is consistent throughout scripture.

In Ephesians 1:12-13, "That we should be to the praise of his glory, who first trusted in Christ. In whom **ye also** *trusted,* **after** that ye **heard the word of truth**, the **gospel of your salvation**: in whom also **after that ye believed,** ye were sealed with that holy Spirit of promise,"

Notice the order:
- They heard the gospel
- They believed and trusted Christ
- The Holy Spirit sealed them.

See also Second Thessalonians 2:13-14.

The concept that a lost person has to be given life, or faith, or something else first before he can believe is not taught in scripture.

10. GOD'S CHOOSING IS NOT BASED ON HIS FOREKNOWLEDGE

The error:

Election is not based on anything God saw in the future. God's foreknowledge means He determined

100   TIPTOE THROUGH THE T-U-L-I-PS

it to be so, or preordained it.

(This is a subtle attack on the omniscience of God, and on His character, and on the clear teaching of His Word. "Yea, hath God said?")

The scriptural response:

First Peter 1:2, "Elect according to the **foreknowledge** of God…" The word for "foreknowledge" in the Greek is "prognosis." It is from a root word "porrhothen," which means distantly or afar off. "Prognosis" means to predict the probable course or outcome of something. The doctor makes a prognosis of someone's condition, so that he can prescribe the right medicine or treatment. However, "proginosko," which is translated "foreknow" in Romans 8:29, is also translated "foreordained" in First Peter 1:20.

Dr. Henry Morris in his footnotes in his study bible, The Defenders Bible, says that from scripture it is clearly seen that God's "foreknowledge" always comes before "election." First Peter 1:2. He said God's "foreknowledge" always comes before "predestination" also. Romans 8:29

"Elect **according to** the foreknowledge of God…" The word for "according" in the Greek is "kata," which means "pertaining to", or "as touching," or "concerning." In the English it means to "be in agreement with, correspond with, or based upon

but try to keep your balance! 101

the authority of." In simple terms it is saying our election is directly pertaining to, concerning, corresponding to and in agreement with, and is based upon God's foreknowledge. The word "elect" is "eklektos" which means selected or chosen.

The word "predestinate" in the Greek is "pro-orizo" which means, "to limit or determine in advance." In scripture it always has to do with those who are already saved. It never is used in relation to an unbeliever, even one who gets saved later. But as Dr. Morris pointed out, God's "foreknowledge" always comes before His "predestinating."

Could God determine to do something without knowing the results ahead of time? That would limit His omniscience.

"Also, Acts 2:23 speaks of Christ as being delivered to be crucified "by the determinate counsel **and** foreknowledge of God" (It includes both), and Acts 15:18, reveals that "Known unto God are all his works from the beginning of the world." His works surely were not planned merely by His foreknowledge of what they would be. Similarly, God "foreknew" that Israel would be His people (Romans 11:2), yet He later chose them by His own will. It clearly suggests planning ahead of time, not just knowing ahead of time."

We are elected because of what God foreknew, "elect according to foreknowledge." However God's knowing ahead of time can never be separated from His doing ahead of time. But God cannot do anything without His omniscience being a part of it. This would limit an all-knowing God.

In every case where God's planning and predestinating are involved (Acts 2:23), it is also true that those who acted according to His foreknowledge carried out those acts of their own volition.

He promises, "…whosoever shall call upon the name of the Lord shall be saved." (Romans 10:13); yet He also says "…he hath chosen us **in him** before the foundation of the world…" (Ephesians 1:4)."

In Ephesians 1:4 when it says, "…he hath chosen us **in him**…" I believe the "in him" is the plan that God put in motion. Ephesians 2:13 says, "But now in Christ Jesus ye who sometimes were far off are made nigh by the blood of Christ." That's the plan God put in motion. If Calvinism were true, God would not have included the "in him," or "in Christ Jesus," in these verses, and other verses which include "in him" or like terminology, there would be no need.

Here are other examples:

Second Timothy 1:9, "…but according to his own purpose and grace, which was given us **in Christ Jesus** before the world began.,

Ephesians 2:6, "And hath raised *us* up together, and made *us* sit together in heavenly places **in Christ Jesus**:"

but try to keep your balance! **103**

"In him" is also a statement of our position. I believe terms such as, "the called" in Romans 8:28, "the elect," "the church," "the first-born," etc. are all a statement of dignity and position and rank. I also believe it is a statement of possession.

God doesn't have to start something to find out what will happen. God provides for all that could happen before He starts it. Christ is the Lamb that was slain before the foundation of the world. Which came first, God's decree to sacrifice His Son, or His foreknowledge of man's need?

There is no question that God elects, chooses, and calls. There is a disagreement on the methods God chose to do that.

Sir Robert Anderson said, "The scriptural expression 'God's elect'…like 'first-born,' is a title of dignity and privilege, applicable exclusively to the Christian."

D.L. Moody used to say, "The elect are the 'whosoever wills;' the non-elect are the 'whosoever won'ts."

C.L. Daniel said, "The doctrine of unconditional election … takes one of the Lord's sweetest and most gracious teachings and turns it into the most heartless and tyrannical, by making God Himself directly responsible for the doom of every lost sinner."

My belief on election, chosen, and called: God chose a plan to choose out a people for a specific purpose. He also chose the methods He would use

104   TIPTOE THROUGH THE T-U-L-I-PS

to carry out His plan.

I was saved on August 2, 1968 at about 1:00 in the morning. There is not a doubt in my mind that that is when it happened. In July of 1967 I told my brother Denny about salvation. I had been attending a Baptist church and heard all about it. I believed everything they said about my being a sinner and needed to be saved, but I didn't think I was ready yet. If I would have died between that time and August 2, of 1968 there is not a doubt in my mind I would be in hell today. I heard it, I understood it, but I was putting off making a decision. Thank God my brother Denny didn't put it off. He got saved right away. He died that winter. Denny is in heaven today. I understood salvation and told him how to do it and I wasn't even saved. I was an unsaved evangelist. I think there might be a few of those on TV.

IV. Calvinism attacks the character of God and the integrity of His Word.

God is a **just** God. He never operates unjustly. Psalm 145:17

Calvinism shows God as a God who:

- Has compassion on some, but not on others.
- Intentionally bypasses some, and allows them to spend eternity in hell without ever really having a chance.

but try to keep your balance! 105

- Has the ability to save all, but chooses not to.

Is this the God of the Bible?

God has limited Himself in His Sovereignty, for He cannot act contrary to His nature, which involves such attributes as His truth, holiness, righteousness, and love.

Does God make a husband love his wife? God's standard is, "Husbands love your wives;" but whether or not he does is a matter of **choice**. Whenever God gives a command, He **always** gives us the ability to obey.

V. Scriptures Calling For Special Attention

Acts 13:48, "...as many as were **ordained** to eternal life believed."

The normal word for ordained is "horizo," which means "to appoint, decree, specify, declare, determine, limit, ordain."

Ex: Acts 10:42, "...was **ordained** of God *to be* the Judge of..."

Acts 17:31, "...by *that* man whom he hath **ordained**..." But that is not the word God chose for Acts 13:48. He chose the word "tasso" instead. "Tasso" means "to arrange in an orderly manner, assign, dispose." It is used only one other time in the New Testament, in Romans 13:1, "...the powers that be are ordained of God."

Second Thessalonians 2:13, "...God hath from the beginning **chosen** you to salvation..."

The word for "chosen" in this verse is also not the normal Greek word that is used. The Greek word used for "select" or "choose out" is "eklegomal." But the word God chose for this verse is "haireomal." This is the only place in the New Testament it is used in this meaning.

There is some uncertainty about what the term "from the beginning" means. Many believe it looks back to the time when God's call through the gospel reached the Thessalonians.

Let's look at the context of this verse to determine its meaning. The unbelievers perish because they "received not the love of the truth, that they might be saved" (verse 10) (To receive something takes an act of the will), and "believe not the truth" in (verse 11). Those who were "chosen," did so because of the work of the Holy Spirit, and the "belief of the truth." (verse 13) They were called to "the obtaining of the glory of our Lord Jesus Christ" Paul says, "by our gospel." (verse 14) Paul points out in (verse 12) that God would damn those who "believed not the truth, but had pleasure in unrighteousness."

It is clear from the text, to make this an arbitrary choosing on God's part, and not based on acceptance or rejection of the gospel would be clearly taking it out of context.

CHAPTER NINE

Dear Calvinistic Friend

Do you believe God in His Sovereignty, because of His Omniscience, could design a plan whereby He could redeem fallen mankind, that would allow man to have a free will, but still allow Himself to be in control? If you believe God is omniscient, and that nothing is impossible with God, then your answer should be an emphatic yes, He could do that. Do you believe that God did design a plan like that? If you have accepted the teachings of Calvin, your answer is probably an emphatic no. I believe that not only could God design a plan like that, I believe He did design a plan like that. So we both probably believe He could design such a plan, you just don't believe He did. Maybe your real problem is a matter of faith, and because of human reasoning

108   TIPTOE THROUGH THE T-U-L-I-PS

you are just limiting God in His Sovereignty.

God's decisions are never based only on our decisions. Before God ever put His plan in motion He knew what our decisions would be. But He formed the plan, knew what the results would be, then put it in motion. Our decisions that would come later were merely a result of the decisions and planning that God did in eternity past. His decisions determined our decisions, yet God in His Sovereignty and Wisdom had a plan that would not violate our freedom of choice, but still left Him in control. That goes against our human reasoning, but I think it is a logical conclusion based on scripture.

A Calvinist believes the reason a person receives the gospel message and is saved, is because they were chosen; if they reject the gospel it is because they were not chosen.

The Bible indicates the reason a person is chosen is because they received the gospel; if they are not chosen it is because they rejected the gospel. Which belief system is based on scripture, and which belief system is based on the teaching of a man?

Calvinists believe God is Sovereign, which is clearly taught in scripture. Calvinists take it one step further and believe therefore man cannot really have a free will, which is clearly not taught in scripture.

Arminians believe man has a free will, which is clearly taught in scripture. Arminians take it one

but try to keep your balance! 109

step further and believe that man's free will after he is saved can cause him to lose his salvation, which clearly is not taught in scripture.

Satan deceived people such as John Calvin, and Arminians such as John Wesley, into bringing in another Jesus, another spirit, and another gospel, and their minds became corrupted from the simplicity that is in Christ. (Second Corinthians 11:3-4) The Apostle Paul feared that would happen, Calvinism and Arminianism are just two of the ways it has. Things that are different are not the same.

I believe whosoever means **whosoever**, in Greek, Hebrew or English. When God said He was not willing that any should perish, He meant just that. When God said He loved the whole world, I believe He loved the whole world. When Jesus spoke of children and said it was not the will of the father that any of these little ones should perish, I think He meant just that. When Jesus cried over Jerusalem and urged His disciples to pray for workers, I think His desire was for all to be saved. That's why I think it broke His heart and moved Him to tears when He said, "but ye would not."

Calvinism is a false doctrine that is a subtle Satanic attack on the Person and work of Jesus Christ, the Person and work of the Holy Spirit, and the simplicity of the gospel; which also attacks the integrity and authority of the very Word of God.

CHAPTER TEN

The Tale of Two Systems

THE PARABLE OF THE SNOW-COVERED DRIVEWAY

A man once decided if he ever had a family, he was only going to love some of his children and not the others. One day, after he had had five sons (all of which were now in their teens), he called them aside and said to them, "Boys, the driveway is covered with snow and needs to be shoveled out. I have divided the driveway into five sections, and each of you will be responsible for his own section. If you take the shovel that I provide for you and shovel out your section, you will be rewarded. If you do not, you will be punished, and I am going to withhold from you your share of my inheritance.

However, he only gave shovels to two of the

112 TIPTOE THROUGH THE T-U-L-I-PS

boys, and withheld them from the others. He did this not because of anything good or bad that was in the boys, or because of anything they had done; but because long before they were born he had decided he would only love his first and third child, and would withhold from the others the shovels that would enable them to fulfill their responsibility to him.

He also planned he would assist the two that he gave shovels to, thereby guaranteeing they would be able to fulfill their obligation. (Whether he actually purchased shovels for all five to begin with has been debated.)

When one of the boys tried to complain, he responded, "Who are you to tell me what I can or cannot do? If it were not for me you would not even exist. You disobeyed me, you deserve to be punished, and I can do with my inheritance as I please."

THE END

That doesn't really sound fair does it? But did you know some people actually believe our Heavenly Father works that way?

Total Inability
None of the boys had shovels at first.

but try to keep your balance! 113

Unconditional Election
The father decided before they were born which children he would love.

Limited Atonement
The father decided he would only love and provide for two.

Irresistible Grace
Accepting or rejecting the shovels didn't enter into it.

Perseverance of the Saints
He guaranteed their success by giving them the ability or help to persevere and finish the job.

THE PARABLE OF THE GREAT DINNER PARTY

A rich man decided to prepare a great dinner party. He decided also that he would only invite poor people who do not have the right clothes to wear, the financial resources to help pay for the dinner or purchase tickets, and the transportation to get them there.

He tells them they cannot come to the dinner party unless they have on the right clothes, but not to worry because he promised to provide them with the clothing himself. He also promised to provide

114   Tiptoe Through the T-U-L-I-Ps

transportation, all they would have to do is just accept the invitation and he would take care of all the rest. But some people turned down the invitation, each for their own reasons, and decided not to come.

Once he knew who had accepted his invitations, and who had rejected them, he made sure that everything was provided for those who were coming to his party.

Even though many accepted his invitation, he still did not have to provide everything for them. They were still poor people who did not have the means to come by themselves, and were depending completely on the provisions and goodness of the rich man. But they all knew he was a kind man who always kept his word. They knew they could trust completely in his promises to them.

THE END

Some of you may have already recognized some similarities between this parable, and one that is recorded in the Bible. God has not only provided a great dinner party, but has also promised that everyone who accepts His invitation to attend, will never again have to go back into their poverty. And not only that, but He has also promised that once we have accepted His invitation, He will make sure that

but try to keep your balance! 115

all our needs are taken care of, right up until the day of the party.

He has promised that if we accept His free invitation, and will take Him at His word, we shall be joint-heirs with His Son, and shall rule with Him in His kingdom.

God has said that in order to come to His party, we have to be clothed in perfect righteousness, which none of us have. But God has provided the clothing Himself, through the righteousness of His Son.

The clothing has been provided, the way has been provided (through acceptance of His Son's death on our behalf), the invitations have been extended ("Whosoever will may come"). Which will it be for us, wealth or poverty?

"For with the heart man believeth unto righteousness; and with the mouth confession is made unto salvation ... For whosoever shall call upon the name of the Lord shall be saved." (Romans 10:10,13)

"...Believe on the Lord Jesus Christ and thou shalt be saved..." (Acts 16:31)